LIFE PICTURE PUZZLE

WELCOME TO LIFE'S SIXTH
PICTURE PUZZLE BOOK

Animals. Americans share their lives with over 120 million cats and dogs, as well as countless other pets. Animals help anchor us to nature; they delight and surprise us, they link us to our past, and, of course, they feed and clothe many of us. Without them, we might not survive. If we did, our lives would be poorer for their lack.

With all this in mind, our team at LIFE happily dedicated our second themed book to the study of all creatures, great and small. Our photo editors searched worldwide for beautiful and amusing pictures of animals in our homes, in our lives, and in the wild. Then, we lovingly turned those photos into our famous puzzles. We hope you enjoy our Animals Picture Puzzle book as much as we enjoyed creating it.

We have endeavored, in this latest book, to keep everything you know and love about our earlier efforts in place. We still start with the Novice section for our first-time readers, and then slowly ratchet up the difficulty with our Master and Expert puzzles. For our most experienced and dedicated puzzlers, we top things off with our Genius puzzles, which are guaranteed to challenge you. Finally, our Classics section brings you some great black-and-white puzzles, using LIFE's amazing and world-famous photo archive.

If you're one of those readers who burn through our puzzles in a few nights, don't fret. Our photo editors are already gathering pictures for our seventh book. When the nights get longer, the days grow colder, and the leaves begin to fall, you'll be able to curl up next to a warm fire with our Holidays Picture Puzzle book. Until then, let us know what you think of our Animals book at picturepuzzle@life.com. We always love to hear from you.

[OUR CUT-UP PUZZLES: EASY AS 1-2-3]

We snipped a photo into 4 or 6 pieces. Then we rearranged the pieces and numbered them.

Your mission: Beneath each cut-up puzzle, write the number of the piece in the box where it belongs.

Check the answer key at the back of the book to see what the reassembled image looks like.

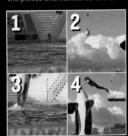

Holidays Picture Puzzle Preview! We know you're impatient for our next book, so we've given you a special sneak preview, a single Holidays Picture Puzzle just for you on the last page of this book. Take your time, work through each Animals puzzle, and then enjoy this special treat. It's a promise of things to come. And remember, you can catch our LIFE Picture Puzzles each month in our sister publication, *All You* magazine.

[HOW TO PLAY THE PUZZLES]

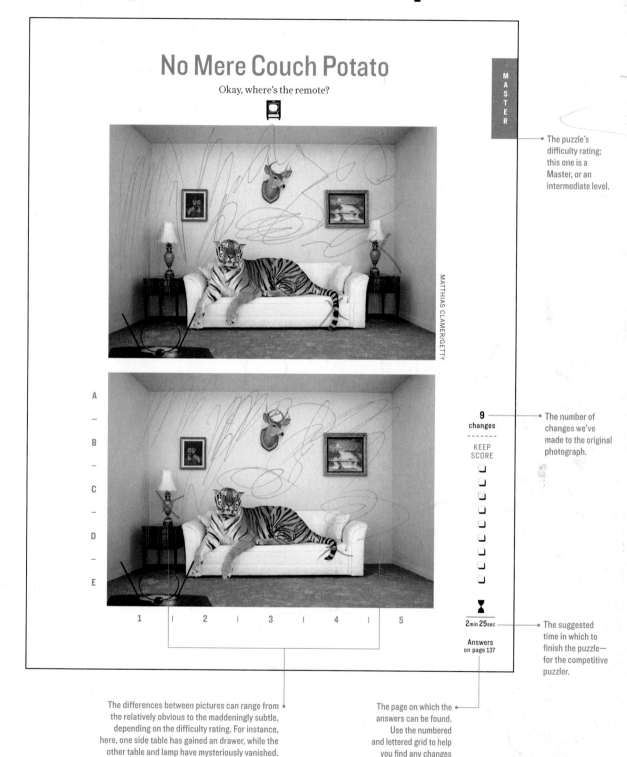

No Mere Couch Potato

Okay, where's the remote?

MASTER

The puzzle's difficulty rating; this one is a Master, or an intermediate level.

9 changes

KEEP SCORE

The number of changes we've made to the original photograph.

2 min 25 sec

Answers on page 137

The suggested time in which to finish the puzzle—for the competitive puzzler.

The differences between pictures can range from the relatively obvious to the maddeningly subtle, depending on the difficulty rating. For instance, here, one side table has gained a drawer, while the other table and lamp have mysteriously vanished. Seven more changes are left to spot in this puzzle.

The page on which the answers can be found. Use the numbered and lettered grid to help you find any changes you might have missed.

LIFE PICTURE PUZZLE

Puzzle Master Michael Roseman
Editor Robert Sullivan
Director of Photography Barbara Baker Burrows
Deputy Picture Editor Christina Lieberman
Research Editor Danny Freedman
Copy Parlan McGaw (Chief), Barbara Gogan, Peter Lucas
Photo Assistant Forrester Hambrecht

LIFE Puzzle Books
Managing Editor Bill Shapiro

LIFE Books
President Andrew Blau
Business Manager Roger Adler
Business Development Manager Jeff Burak

Editorial Operations
Richard K. Prue, David Sloan (Directors), Richard Shaffer (Group Manager),
Brian Fellows, Raphael Joa, Angel Mass, Stanley E. Moyse, Albert Rufino (Managers),
Soheila Asayesh, Keith Aurelio, Trang Ba Chuong, Charlotte Coco, Osmar Escalona,
Kevin Hart, Norma Jones, Mert Kerimoglu, Rosalie Khan, Marco Lau, Po Fung Ng,
Rudi Papiri, Barry Pribula, Carina A. Rosario, Christopher Scala, Diana Suryakusuma,
Vaune Trachtman, Paul Tupay, Lionel Vargas, David Weiner

Time Inc. Home Entertainment
Publisher Richard Fraiman
General Manager Steven Sandonato
Executive Director, Marketing Services Carol Pittard
Director, Retail & Special Sales Tom Mifsud
Director, New Product Development Peter Harper
Assistant Director, Brand Marketing Laura Adam
Associate Counsel Helen Wan
Senior Brand Manager, TWRS/M Holly Oakes
Book Production Manager Suzanne Janso
Design & Prepress Manager Anne-Michelle Gallero
Senior Brand Manager Joy Butts
Brand Manager Shelley Rescober

Special thanks to Alexandra Bliss, Glenn Buonocore, Susan Chodakiewicz, Margaret Hess,
Robert Marasco, Dennis Marcel, Brooke Reger, Mary Sarro-Waite, Ilene Schreider,
Adriana Tierno, Alex Voznesenskiy

PUBLISHED BY

LIFE Books

Vol. 8, No. 7 • July 7, 2008

Copyright 2008
Time Inc.
1271 Avenue of the Americas
New York, New York 10020

We welcome your comments and suggestions about LIFE Books. Please write to us at:
LIFE Books
Attention: Book Editors
PO Box 11016
Des Moines, IA 50336-1016

If you would like to order any of our hardcover Collector's Edition books, please call us at 1-800-327-6388 (Monday through Friday, 7 a.m. to 8 p.m., or Saturday, 7 a.m. to 6 p.m. Central Time).

READY, SET, GO!

NOVI

CE [

These puzzles are for everyone:
rookies and veterans,
young and old. Start here, and
sharpen your skills.

]

Udderly at Home

The milk is in the fridge

CATHERINE LEDNER/GETTY

A

B

C

D

E

1   2   3   4   5

6
changes

KEEP
SCORE

⧗

2min 10sec

Answers
on page 137

Shh! Did You Hear Something?

Let's stay as quiet as a ... hamster

A
—
B
—
C
—
D
—
E

1   2   3   4   5

9
changes

⏳
2min 50sec

Answers
on page 137

KEEP SCORE ★ ❑ ❑ ❑ ❑ ❑ ❑ ❑ ❑ ❑

Monkeyshines

Our simian friend makes like Tiger

2min 55sec

Answers
on page 137

A

B

C

D

E

1   2   3   4   5

Split Personality

He's having quite an identity crisis

A
—
B
—
C
—
D
—
E

1 | 2 | 3 | 4 | 5

10
changes

3min 40sec

Answers
on page 137

KEEP SCORE ★ ❏ ❏ ❏ ❏ ❏ ❏ ❏ ❏ ❏ ❏

Don't Hold the Lettuce

If there isn't enough to go around,
the bunnies are going to be hopping mad

ZHOU QINGXIAN/CHINAFOTOPRESS

9
changes

⧗

3min 20sec

Answers
on page 137

KEEP SCORE ★ ❑ ❑ ❑ ❑ ❑ ❑ ❑ ❑ ❑ ❑

Pride Before a Fall

One giant leap for lion-kind

8
changes

- - - - - - -

KEEP
SCORE

❏
❏
❏
❏
❏
❏
❏
❏

⧗

3min 15sec

Answers
on page 137

A
—
B
—
C
—
D
—
E

1   2   3   4   5

Geek of the North

We hope he's in a wireless hotspot

WAYNE R. BILENDUKE/GETTY

A
—
B
—
C
—
D
—
E

1 | 2 | 3 | 4 | 5

7
changes

⧗

3min 40sec

Answers
on page 137

KEEP SCORE ★ ❑ ❑ ❑ ❑ ❑ ❑ ❑

Open Wide, Please

Watch your fingers while you try to solve this one

9
changes

KEEP
SCORE

A
B
C
D
E

⧗
3min 10sec

Answers
on page 137

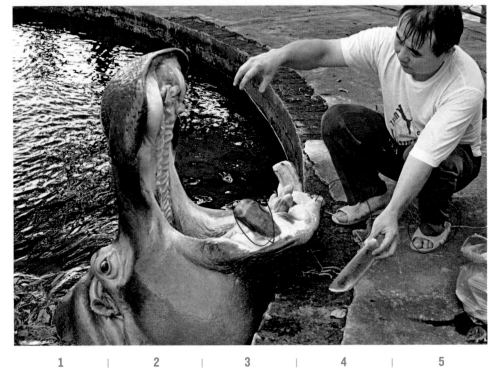

1 2 3 4 5

Is That for Me?

The big fella's got a sweet tooth

JEFF BURAK

A
—
B
—
C
—
D
—
E

1   2   3   4   5

7
changes

- - - - - - - - -

KEEP
SCORE

❑
❑
❑
❑
❑
❑
❑

⧖

3min 20sec

Answers
on page 137

Now Boarding

This hairy beast is just about ready for departure

JAMES BURROWS

A

B

C

D

E

1   2   3   4   5

10 changes

⧗

2min 55sec

Answers on page 137

KEEP SCORE ★ ❑ ❑ ❑ ❑ ❑ ❑ ❑ ❑ ❑ ❑

Where's Fido?

Everybody, keep sniffing. He's got to be here somewhere.

GK HART & VIKKI HART/GETTY

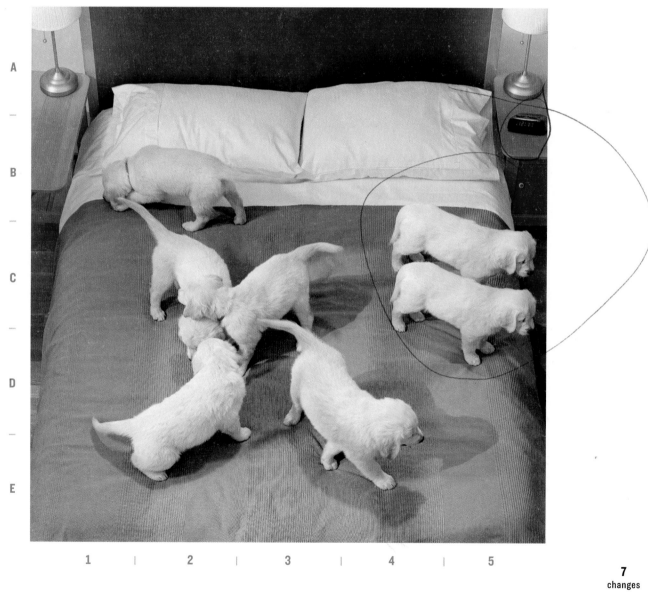

A —

B —

C —

D —

E

1 | 2 | 3 | 4 | 5

7
changes

⧗
2min 40sec

Answers
on page 138

KEEP SCORE ★ ❑ ❑ ❑ ❑ ❑ ❑ ❑

Study Hard, Cubbie

Otherwise, it's a jungle out there

FREDERICK FLORIN/GETTY

A
B
C
D
E

1   2   3   4   5

8
changes

⧗
2min 30sec

Answers
on page 138

KEEP SCORE ★ ❏ ❏ ❏ ❏ ❏ ❏ ❏ ❏

G'day, Mate

These guys will jump for treats

ZHOU QINGXIAN/CHINAFOTOPRESS

10
changes

- - - - - - - - -

KEEP
SCORE

❏
❏
❏
❏
❏
❏
❏
❏
❏
❏

⧖

3min 45sec

Answers
on page 138

A

—

B

—

C

—

D

—

E

1   2   3   4   5

Once Upon a Time . . .

. . . there were three little kitties

MARIE DUBRACL/GETTY

9
changes

- - - - - - - -

KEEP
SCORE

☐
☐
☐
☐
☐
☐
☐
☐
☐

⌛
3min 20sec

Answers
on page 138

Giving Thanks

No table scraps for these two

A

B

C

10 changes

KEEP SCORE

D

E

3min 25sec

Answers on page 138

1 | 2 | 3 | 4 | 5

Swan Lake

Which one of these ducky photos is just a little different?

1

2

3

4

5

6

0min 20sec

Answer
on page 138

FRANS LEMMENS/GETTY

To Everything, Tern, Tern, Tern

Don't be gulled into thinking all six photos are the same

1

2

3

4

5

DAVID ATTWOOD

6

0min 15sec

Answer
on page 138

Creature Comforts

Check out this purr-fect home away from home

JUSTIN SULLIVAN/GETTY

11
changes

KEEP
SCORE

☐ ☐ ☐ ☐ ☐ ☐ ☐ ☐ ☐ ☐ ☐

⏳

3min 55sec

Answers
on page 138

A | B | C | D | E

1 | 2 | 3 | 4 | 5

You've Got Mail

Staying in touch has never been easier

9
changes

KEEP
SCORE

❏
❏
❏
❏
❏
❏
❏
❏
❏

⌛

3min 35sec

Answers
on page 138

Tree Hugger

Who can put Froggy together again?

0min 25sec

Answer
on page 138

KEEP SCORE

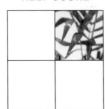

On Thin Ice

Time to get your ducks in order

KEEP SCORE

0min 30sec

Answer
on page 138

Strange Bedfellows

It's going to take a birdie to make the felines smile

A   B   C   D   E

11
changes

- - - - - - - - - -

KEEP
SCORE

❏
❏
❏
❏
❏
❏
❏
❏
❏
❏
❏

⧗

4min 5sec

Answers
on page 138

MAST

ER[ ]

Here, puzzles get
a little harder. You'll
need to raise
your game a level.

Staaay!

This is more temptation than a fellow should have to bear

A
—
B
—
C
—
D
—
E

1 | 2 | 3 | 4 | 5

8
changes

⧗
2min 30sec

Answers
on page 139

KEEP SCORE ★ ❏ ❏ ❏ ❏ ❏ ❏ ❏ ❏

Water Sports

Are you foxy enough to catch our changes?

A
—
B
—
C
—
D
—
E

1 | 2 | 3 | 4 | 5

11
changes

⧗

4min 10sec

Answers
on page 139

KEEP SCORE ★ ❏ ❏ ❏ ❏ ❏ ❏ ❏ ❏ ❏ ❏ ❏

Food and Swine

Keep those groceries at bay

A
—
B
—
C
—
D
—
E

1 | 2 | 3 | 4 | 5

12
changes
- - - - - - - - -
KEEP
SCORE
❑
❑
❑
❑
❑
❑
❑
❑
❑
❑
❑
❑

⧖
4min 15sec

Answers
on page 139

Just Call Him Spike

He's keeping his eyes on you—all three of them

1

2

3

4

5

6

0min 35sec

Answer
on page 139

MICHAEL AND PATRICIA FOGDEN/GETTY (BOTH PAGES)

A Mother's Work Is Never Done

Can birds hire daycare?

0min 45sec

Answer
on page 139

Choose Me!

Well, maybe that's not what they're saying

RYAN MESINA

A
—
B
—
C
—
D
—
E

1 | 2 | 3 | 4 | 5

10
changes

3min 50sec

Answers
on page 139

KEEP SCORE ★ ❏ ❏ ❏ ❏ ❏ ❏ ❏ ❏ ❏ ❏

Off and Running

This one's a real obstacle course

A
—
B
—
C
—
D
—
E

1 | 2 | 3 | 4 | 5

8
changes

⧖
3min 35sec

Answers
on page 139

KEEP SCORE ★ ❏ ❏ ❏ ❏ ❏ ❏ ❏ ❏

Panda-monium

It's always playtime at the zoo

WANG XIWEI/CHINAFOTOPRESS

A
—
B
—
C
—
D
—
E

1 | 2 | 3 | 4 | 5

11
changes
- - - - - - - - -
KEEP
SCORE
❑
❑
❑
❑
❑
❑
❑
❑
❑
❑
❑

⏳
3min 55sec

Answers
on page 139

Oops!

Honest, I was just looking for my dog bone

THOMAS JACKSON/GETTY

10
changes

KEEP
SCORE

☐
☐
☐
☐
☐
☐
☐
☐
☐
☐

⌛

4min 5sec

Answers
on page 139

A
—
B
—
C
—
D
—
E

1 | 2 | 3 | 4 | 5

Finding Nemo ...

... and his friends in a watery wonderland

GEORGETTE DOUWMA/GETTY

A
—
B
—
C
—
D
—
E

1 | 2 | 3 | 4 | 5

12
changes
- - - - - - - -
KEEP
SCORE

☐
☐
☐
☐
☐
☐
☐
☐
☐
☐
☐
☐

⏳
4min 15sec

Answers
on page 139

You From Around Here?

I'm just trying to find the pyramids. Any ideas?

A
—
B
—
C
—
D
—
E

1 | 2 | 3 | 4 | 5

10 changes

4min 20sec

Answers
on page 139

KEEP SCORE ★ ❑ ❑ ❑ ❑ ❑ ❑ ❑ ❑ ❑ ❑

Clowning Around

Life is a circus for these pooches

A

B

C

D

E

1 | 2 | 3 | 4 | 5

12
changes

- - - - - - - - -

KEEP
SCORE

⌐⌐
⌐⌐
⌐⌐
⌐⌐
⌐⌐
⌐⌐
⌐⌐
⌐⌐
⌐⌐
⌐⌐

⌛

4min 35sec

Answers
on page 139

Thundering Herd

They're doing their best not to be on the menu tonight

A
—
B
—
C
—
D
—
E

1 | 2 | 3 | 4 | 5

10
changes

4min 50sec

Answers
on page 140

KEEP SCORE ★ ❑ ❑ ❑ ❑ ❑ ❑ ❑ ❑ ❑ ❑

He's Got a Thick Hide

And that's a good thing for his passengers

JAMES BURROWS

A
—
B
—
C
—
D
—
E

1 | 2 | 3 | 4 | 5

12
changes

⧖
4min 50sec

Answers
on page 140

KEEP SCORE ★ ❏ ❏ ❏ ❏ ❏ ❏ ❏ ❏ ❏ ❏ ❏ ❏

See Spot Run, Sort Of

We've milked this one for all it's worth

A
–
B
–
C
–
D
–
E

1 | 2 | 3 | 4 | 5

11 changes

⧗
4min 40sec

Answers
on page 140

KEEP SCORE ★ ❏ ❏ ❏ ❏ ❏ ❏ ❏ ❏ ❏ ❏ ❏

Don't Get Crabby

Just put your pincers on the photo that's been changed

1

2

3

4

5

6

1min 20sec

Answer
on page 140

JOSEPH VAN OS/GETTY

Slithering Serpents

One of these pictures is squirmingly different

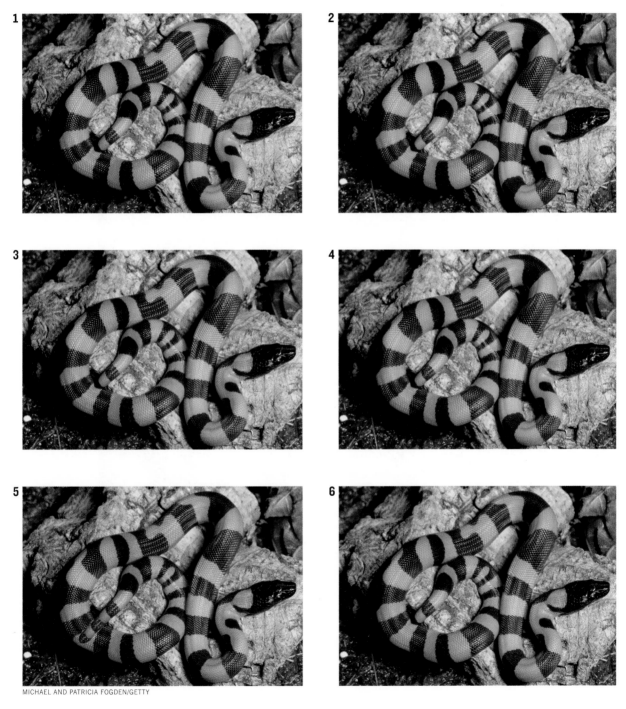

MICHAEL AND PATRICIA FOGDEN/GETTY

1min 35sec

Answer
on page 140

Leader of the Pack

Let's go, let's go, let's go, let's go

A
–
B
–
C
–
D
–
E

1 | 2 | 3 | 4 | 5

8
changes

KEEP
SCORE

❏
❏
❏
❏
❏
❏
❏
❏

⧗
3min 55sec

Answers
on page 140

These Ruins Need Fixing

You don't have to be Indiana Jones to solve this

⧗ 1 min 15 sec

Answer on page 140

KEEP SCORE

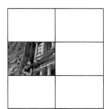

A Ruff One

Help these doggies complete their call

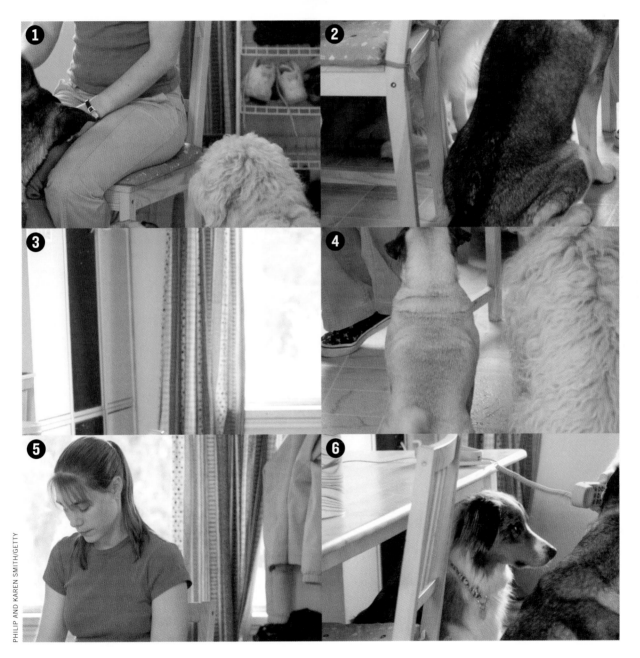

PHILIP AND KAREN SMITH/GETTY

KEEP SCORE

⧖
1min 5sec

Answer
on page 140

It's Lunchtime

Oh, no, not fish again!

TUI DE ROY/GETTY

5

4

3

2

1

A | B | C | D | E

11
changes
- - - - - - - - -
KEEP
SCORE

❏ ❏ ❏ ❏ ❏ ❏ ❏ ❏ ❏ ❏ ❏

⏳

4min **55**sec

Answers
on page 140

EXPE

RT [

Only serious puzzlers
dare to tread past this point.
Who's in?
]

One Horse Power

This puzzle's a little buggy

ED FREEMAN/GETTY

A
—
B
—
C
—
D
—
E

1   2   3   4   5

13
changes

5min 25sec

Answers
on page 140

KEEP SCORE ★ ❑ ❑ ❑ ❑ ❑ ❑ ❑ ❑ ❑ ❑ ❑ ❑ ❑

Snakes in the Grass

There's about to be a rumble in this jungle

A
—
B
—
C
—
D
—
E

1   2   3   4   5

8
changes

5min 10sec

Answers
on page 140

KEEP SCORE ★ ❑ ❑ ❑ ❑ ❑ ❑ ❑ ❑

Don't Feed the Bears

"Oh, c'mon—my stomach's growling!"

DOUG ALLAN/GETTY

A

B

C

D

E

1   2   3   4   5

12
changes

- - - - - - - - -

KEEP
SCORE

❏
❏
❏
❏
❏
❏
❏
❏
❏
❏
❏
❏

⌛

5min 15sec

Answers
on page 141

Idita-ready?

These huskies will be in shape when the snow falls

THEO HEIMANN/GETTY

A

B

C

D

E

1　　　2　　　3　　　4　　　5

10
changes

5min 5sec

Answers
on page 141

KEEP SCORE ★ ❏ ❏ ❏ ❏ ❏ ❏ ❏ ❏ ❏ ❏

Hands Off My Food

Everything's up for grabs here

A

B

C

D

E

1   2   3   4   5

13
changes

KEEP
SCORE

❏
❏
❏
❏
❏
❏
❏
❏
❏
❏
❏
❏
❏

⏳

5min 15sec

Answers
on page 141

Swimming Lessons

Care to take a quack at this one?

THOMAS KITCHIN AND VICTORIA HURST /GETTY

9
changes

- - - - - - - - -

KEEP
SCORE

☐
☐
☐
☐
☐
☐
☐
☐
☐

⏳

4min 45sec

Answers
on page 141

A
—
B
—
C
—
D
—
E

1 | 2 | 3 | 4 | 5

Shell Game

She always looks good for her public

A

—

B

—

C

—

D

—

E

1   2   3   4   5

10
changes

- - - - - - - - -

KEEP
SCORE

❏
❏
❏
❏
❏
❏
❏
❏
❏

⧗

4min 40sec

Answers
on page 141

Farm Fresh

Things are changing for this family of redheads

9
changes

KEEP
SCORE

❏
❏
❏
❏
❏
❏
❏
❏
❏

⏳

4min 35sec

Answers
on page 141

You Looking at Me?

With his eyesight, it's easy to tell which picture's different

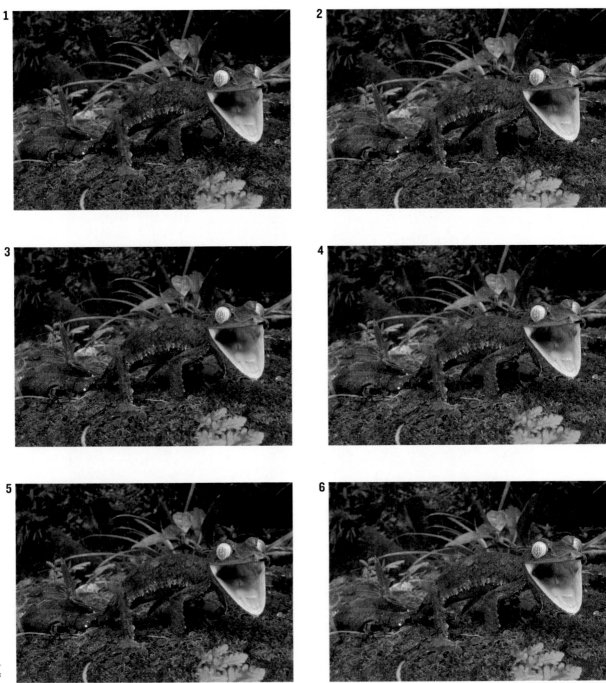

1 | 2

3 | 4

5 | 6

1min 40sec

Answer
on page 141

PIOTR NASKRECKI/GETTY

And Baby Makes Three

One's different, but just by a neck

1

2

3

4

5

6

GONG HUI/CHINAFOTOPRESS

1min 30sec

Answer
on page 141

Walk This Way

Please obey all traffic regulations

GETTY

A

B

C

D

E

1   2   3   4   5

12
changes
- - - - - - - - -
KEEP
SCORE

❏
❏
❏
❏
❏
❏
❏
❏
❏
❏
❏
❏

⌛

5min 30sec

Answers
on page 141

Last One In Is Whale Food

Get those happy feet ready to run

COLIN MONTEATH/GETTY

11
changes

- - - - - - - -

KEEP
SCORE

❏
❏
❏
❏
❏
❏
❏
❏
❏
❏
❏

⌛

5min 10sec

Answers
on page 141

A
—
B
—
C
—
D
—
E

1 | 2 | 3 | 4 | 5

Little Nipper Napping

He's sleeping through a Disney moment

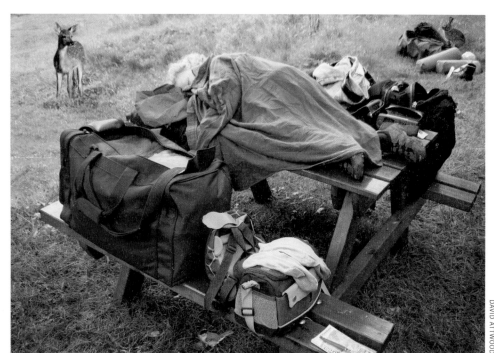

DAVID ATTWOOD

12
changes

KEEP
SCORE

⏳

4min 55sec

Answers
on page 141

Summertime...

...and the living is easy

RYAN MESINA

15
changes

- - - - - - - - -

KEEP
SCORE

❑ ❑ ❑ ❑ ❑ ❑ ❑ ❑ ❑ ❑ ❑ ❑ ❑ ❑ ❑

⌛

5min 55sec

Answers
on page 142

GENI

JS[ ]

Finding a single difference
in these puzzles is a
challenge. Finding them all
might be impossible.

Mr. Zippy

Anyway, he's faster than a speeding snail

GEORGE GRALL/GETTY

A
—
B
—
C
—
D
—
E

1   2   3   4   5

15
changes

⧗
5min 30sec

Answers
on page 142

KEEP SCORE ★ ❑ ❑ ❑ ❑ ❑ ❑ ❑ ❑ ❑ ❑ ❑ ❑ ❑ ❑ ❑

Wool Gathering

Separate yourself from the herd on this one

16
changes
- - - - - - - - -
KEEP
SCORE

☐
☐
☐
☐
☐
☐
☐
☐
☐
☐
☐
☐
☐
☐
☐
☐

⧖

5min 15sec

Answers
on page 142

Run Away!

At the finish, it's Funky Hat by a nose!

YU ZHIYONG/CHINAFOTOPRESS

14
changes

- - - - - - - -

KEEP
SCORE

5min 5sec

Answers
on page 142

A

B

C

D

E

1   2   3   4   5

Practical Yoke

This one requires team effort

FRANS LEMMENS/GETTY

A
—
B
—
C
—
D
—
E

1   2   3   4   5

16
changes

KEEP
SCORE

☐
☐
☐
☐
☐
☐
☐
☐
☐
☐
☐
☐
☐
☐

⌛

5min 25sec

Answers
on page 142

Monkey on His Back

Creating these puzzles is a burden we're happy to shoulder

JOHN LUND/GETTY

20
changes

- - - - - - - - -

KEEP
SCORE

⧗
6min 5sec

Answers
on page 142

A | B | C | D | E

1   2   3   4   5

Launching

Or just lunching?

A

B

C

D

E

1   2   3   4   5

15
changes
- - - - - - - -
KEEP
SCORE

❏
❏
❏
❏
❏
❏
❏
❏
❏
❏
❏
❏
❏
❏
❏

⏳
5min 40sec

Answers
on page 142

Crowded House

We've heard about sharing the office, but this is ridiculous

A

B

17
changes

KEEP
SCORE

❑
❑
❑
❑
❑
❑
❑
❑
❑
❑
❑
❑
❑
❑
❑
❑
❑

C

⏳

5min 45sec

D

Answers
on page 142

E

1 | 2 | 3 | 4 | 5

Knock, Knock—Anyone Home?

There's no more room at this inn.

ART MONTES DE OCA/GETTY

19
changes

- - - - - - - - -

KEEP
SCORE

⌛
5min 55sec

Answers
on page 142

LIFE CLASS

ICS[

These puzzles were
specially created with
memorable photos
from the LIFE archives.

]

Tweetie Birds

These little darlings are happy to flock together

NINA LEEN/LIFE

A
—
B
—
C
—
D
—
E

1 | 2 | 3 | 4 | 5

9
changes

3min 30sec

Answers
on page 143

KEEP SCORE ★ ❑ ❑ ❑ ❑ ❑ ❑ ❑ ❑ ❑

Who Needs a Spoon?

But you have to be careful of brain freeze

8
changes

- - - - - - - -

KEEP
SCORE

❑
❑
❑
❑
❑
❑
❑
❑

⏳

3min 50sec

Answers
on page 143

A
—
B
—
C
—
D
—
E

1 | 2 | 3 | 4 | 5

Don't Spook the Ponies

As if that were possible

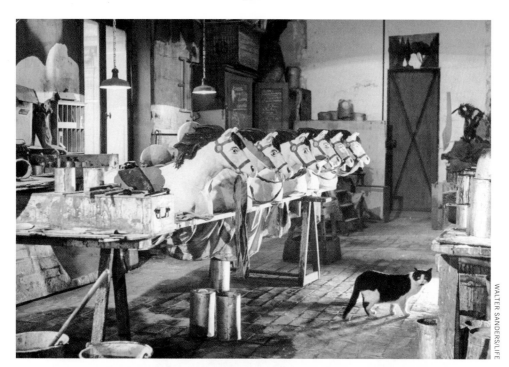

WALTER SANDERS/LIFE

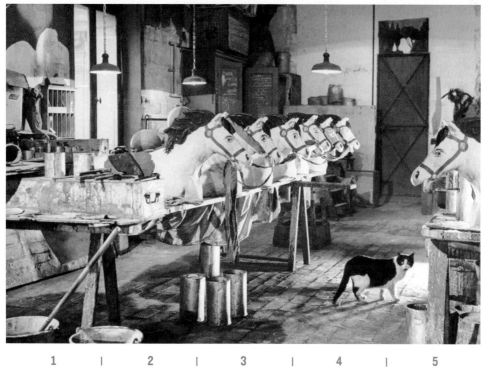

A
—
B
—
C
—
D
—
E

1 | 2 | 3 | 4 | 5

10
changes
- - - - - - -
KEEP
SCORE

❏
❏
❏
❏
❏
❏
❏
❏
❏
❏

⧗
4min 15sec

Answers
on page 143

Making a Splash

Flipper's got nothing on this charismatic fellow

A
—
B
—
C
—
D
—
E

1 | 2 | 3 | 4 | 5

9
changes
- - - - - - - - -
KEEP
SCORE

4min 45sec

Answers
on page 143

A Maxi Lube Job

Everything's set under the hood (and in the trunk)

11
changes

4min **50**sec

Answers
on page 143

KEEP SCORE ★ ❏ ❏ ❏ ❏ ❏ ❏ ❏ ❏ ❏ ❏ ❏

Weighty Matters

Pound for pound, nothing's cuter

A
—

B
—

C
—

D
—

E

1 | 2 | 3 | 4 | 5

10
changes

4min 20sec

Answers
on page 143

KEEP SCORE ★ ❑ ❑ ❑ ❑ ❑ ❑ ❑ ❑ ❑ ❑

Howdy, Pardners

Guess you won't be needing any gas

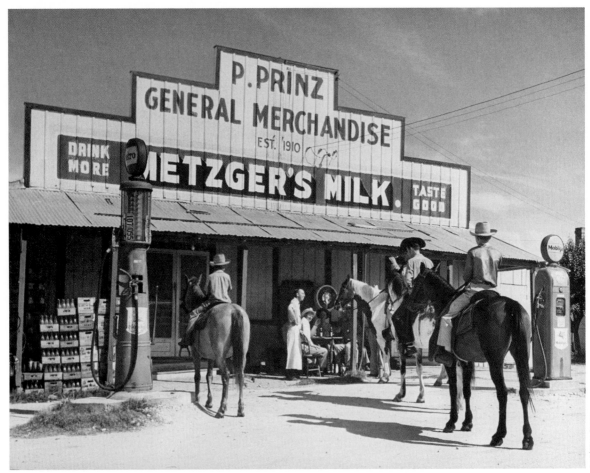

HANS WILD/LIFE

A
—
B
—
C
—
D
—
E

1 | 2 | 3 | 4 | 5

15
changes

5min 10sec

Answers
on page 143

KEEP SCORE ★ ❏ ❏ ❏ ❏ ❏ ❏ ❏ ❏ ❏ ❏ ❏ ❏ ❏ ❏ ❏

Herd Instinct

Directing traffic in the Big Apple

GEORGE SILK/LIFE

12
changes
- - - - - - - -
KEEP
SCORE

❏
❏
❏
❏
❏
❏
❏
❏
❏
❏
❏
❏

⧗

4min 55sec

Answers
on page 143

[ANSWERS]

Finished already? Let's see how you did.

[INTRODUCTION]

Page 3: No Mere Couch Potato No. 1 (A3): These antlers make for quite a rack. No. 2 (B2): Bebé tigre has turned the other cheek. No. 3 (B4): If you paint on rubber instead of canvas, you can stretch the picture whenever you want. No. 4 (C1 to D1): This lamp comes in many colors. No. 5 (C5 to E5): By now, the missing lamp and table are making guest appearances on *Antiques Roadshow*. No. 6 (D1 to D2): Maybe the remote is hiding in the new drawer. No. 7 (D3): His hind leg is even more formidable now. No. 8 (D4 to E4): His tail has been cropped. No. 9 (E2): With a paw this big, he must be a lefty.

[NOVICE]

Page 8: Udderly at Home No. 1 (A1 to B1): Normally, artwork slides down the wall, not up. No. 2 (B3 to C3): The calf has flicked her ear forward. No. 3 (C3): And she's really licking her chops—something must smell good. No. 4 (C4): The door knob has been supersized. No. 5 (E2 to E3): Sure hope she wiped her hooves first. No. 6 (E5): Now, where did that chair go?

Page 10: Shh! Did You Hear Something? No. 1 (A1 to A2): The stem is twisting slowly in the wind. No. 2 (B5): The hamsters have an uninvited guest. No. 3 (B5 to C5): And the rock is a little bloated. No. 4 (C3 to C4): This guy is all ears. No. 5 (D2): With fingers like this, he should play the piano. No. 6 (D2 to D3): Tropical drinks can calm the nerves. No. 7 (E3): Someone dropped an acorn. No. 8 (E3 to E4): Half a leaf is better than none. No. 9 (E4 to E5): Pine needles give off the nicest aroma.

Page 12: Monkeyshines No. 1 (A5 to B4): An elephant is nosing around. No. 2 (B1 to B2): The sleeve is longer and very puffy. No. 3 (B2): The chimp is wearing his Christmas earring. No. 4 (B4): The letter *A* is turning somersaults. No. 5 (C2): The hole has vanished from the green on his shirt. No. 6 (D3): He's wearing stretch socks. Nos. 7 and 8 (D4): The club is broken and its head has spun around. No. 9 (E1 to E3): He's got extra balls for practice shots.

Page 14: Split Personality No. 1 (A2 to A3): A worried emu keeps pacing and pacing. No. 2 (A3 to A4): The drive-by tourist has driven away. No. 3 (A4 to B5): This rail is definitely warped. No. 4 (B1): With a snout like that, he can stick it in anywhere. No. 5 (B3 to C3): These stripes are catching. No. 6 (C1 to C2): The fence is being repaired. No. 7 (C4): One stripe seems to have fallen off. No. 8 (C5 to D5): That's one long tail. No. 9 (D1 to E5): That, um, zorse has lost his shadow. No. 10 (D4 to E4): And he's kicking up a fuss about it.

Page 16: Don't Hold the Lettuce No. 1 (B3): These bunnies trade lettuce for necklaces. No. 2 (B5 to C5): With a hat like this, he must be called Bobby. No. 3 (C2): He's got his starry pants on. No. 4 (C2 to D2): This rabbit has hyper-hearing. No. 5 (C3): They're munching so fast, she's lucky she hasn't lost a finger. No. 6 (C4): The little girl's blouse has been edited. No. 7 (C5): A bunny's popped in from nowhere. No. 8 (D1): He's got a twitchy ear. No. 9 (D5): Blue girls are out this year.

Page 18: Pride Before a Fall No. 1 (A3 to C5): She can leap higher. No. 2 (B1): Somehow the branch is growing. No. 3 (B2): This little birdie is taking a big, big chance. No. 4 (C2 to C3): The cat toy has swung in front of the branch. No. 5 (C3): For dead wood, it moves around quite a bit. No. 6 (D2): The ball is a bit yellow. No. 7 (D4 to E4): Where have these cubs been hiding? No. 8 (E5): And what's happened to Momma?

Page 20: Geek of the North No. 1 (B2): Is he shaking his head at us? No. 2 (C1): That laptop is fast becoming a desktop. No. 3 (C3): The wind has shifted. No. 4 (C3 to D3): The flag dog is sneaking up on the fur coat. No. 5 (C4): The white dog is keeping track of the dogs in front. No. 6 (C4 to E5): These dogs are inching away. No. 7 (D2): Pink is secretly his favorite color.

Page 22: Open Wide, Please No. 1 (A2 to C2): My, what a big mouth you have. No. 2 (A3 to B3): Be careful on the crumbling concrete. No. 3 (B3): The watermelon slice went superfast. No. 4 (C3 to D3): This tooth really chops up melons. No. 5 (C5): His shirt sleeve has sagged. No. 6 (D3): That's another slice down the hatch. No. 7 (D4 to D5): He's wearing some hot sandals. No. 8 (D4 to E4): When it comes to watermelons, bigger is better. No. 9 (E5): This is not the mouse that roared.

Page 23: Is That for Me? No. 1 (A1 to B3): This must be a fun house mirror. No. 2 (A2): It's good to know Al is an American. No. 3 (B3 to B4): Her horns are growing. No. 4 (B4 to C5): And the spots are merging. No. 5 (C4): Candy cane sure beats carrots. No. 6 (D1): He's put on his glasses to get a better view. No. 7 (D3): The tongue is turning pink.

Page 24: Now Boarding No. 1 (A1): A tree grows in China. No. 2 (B1 to B4): Everyone is sure to notice the sign now. No. 3 (B1): Who's been playing with the letters? No. 4 (B1 to B2): The camel has quite a schnoz. No. 5 (B5 to C5): Now there are lots of postcards for sale. No. 6 (C1 to D1): A shop worker has donned a colorful costume. No. 7 (C2 to D2): The camel's lead has slipped behind. No. 8 (D4 to E4): Never trust a three-legged stepladder. No. 9 (D5 to E4): Adding an extra step doesn't make this ladder any safer. No. 10 (E5): Please make sure to hold on to the railing when boarding.

Page 26: Where's Fido? No. 1 (A1): Don't play with the new pull cord. No. 2 (A3): Carpenters are working on the headboard. No. 3 (B1): They've also added on to the night table. No. 4 (B3): He's got a whale of a tail. Nos. 5 and 6 (B5): Now they don't need a wake-up call, and perhaps Fido is behind door number one. No. 7 (C4 to C5): The litter has grown by one.

Page 28: Study Hard, Cubbie No. 1 (A1 to C1): The cub looks ready for graduate school. No. 2 (B3 to C5): Mom's eyes are light sensitive. No. 3 (C1 to C2): "Don't it make his brown eyes blue." No. 4 (C4): And she's camouflaging her nose. No. 5 (D1): His whiskers are still growing. No. 6 (D4): Her nose pad is trying to blend in. No. 7 (E1): She likes us, she really likes us—at least her fur does. No. 8 (E4): It's time to have her beard trimmed.

Page 30: G'Day Mate Nos. 1 and 2 (A1): The lady behind the glass must be making the pigeon flighty. No. 3 (A2): The post wants to be a pillar. No. 4 (A4): He's put a cap on. No. 5 (B2): The kangaroo has vanished. No. 6 (B5): The baby is going to love his toy joey. No. 7 (C4): Always bring a change of socks to the zoo. No. 8 (D1): This curious roo is getting closer. No. 9 (D3 to E3): Somehow, everyone shows up when they think there might be free food. No. 10 (D4 to D5): The landing has been reinforced with more lumber.

Page 31: Once Upon a Time . . . No. 1 (A3 to B3): The seat back is all wicker. No. 2 (A4): The pillow is very pointy. No. 3 (C2): Her dress has one fewer spot. No. 4 (C3): Is this kitty cat wearing blue contacts? No. 5 (C4): One of these pages is a bit swollen. No. 6 (C5 to D5): The teddy bear is getting restless. No. 7 (D2): She's wearing her new bracelet. No. 8 (E2 to E4): Her dress must not be shrink free. No. 9 (E5): The edge of the bench is getting woodier.

Page 32: Giving Thanks No. 1 (A2 to A3): This mirror is worth some reflection. No. 2 (B4 to C4): Who's behind those designer specs? Nos. 3 and 4 (C2): He's so hungry, his tongue is hanging out and his dog-bone tag has turned blue. Nos. 5 and 6 (C4): They've gained an extra pinecone, but he's lost his dog tag. No. 7 (C5): The chair is losing its crisscross. No. 8 (D3): This candleholder towers over the other. No. 9 (E1 to E2): Someone lost his silverware. No. 10 (E4): The noisemaker has a bigger bang.

Page 34: Swan Lake The front swan in photo No. 1 has a big beak.

Page 35: To Everything, Tern, Tern, Tern In photo No. 5, her dolphin logo makes a bold statement.

Page 36: Creature Comforts No. 1 (A1 to B1): Now the cat statue has a friend. No. 2 (A2): They've replaced the mask just in time. No. 3 (A3): The flowers have swapped colors. No. 4 (A3 to A4): This amateur photographer likes to show off her work. No. 5 (A5 to B5): Now this window lets in more light. No. 6 (B2): Wider perches make better sleeping spots. No. 7 (B3 to B4): Each new cat-of-the-day gets his picture on the wall. No. 8 (C2): Let's put the *A* back in ASPCA. No. 9 (C4): She's flicking her tail back and forth. No. 10 (E3): These tiles are now one. No. 11 (E4): Has she forgotten her catnip mouse?

Page 38: You've Got Mail No. 1 (A1 to A3): The door just isn't going to close. No. 2 (A4 to A5): Use this monitor to get the big picture. No. 3 (B3): The screen door has more slats now. No. 4 (B4 to B5): The dog bone has spun around. No. 5 (B5): The postcard is upside down. No. 6 (C1): His collar sports more studs. No. 7 (C5): Whatever you do, don't press the red button. No. 8 (D4 to D5): The mouse has cut the cord. No. 9 (E1): He's losing his spots.

Page 40: Tree Hugger

2	3
1	4

Page 41: On Thin Ice

3	2
4	1

Page 42: Strange Bedfellows No. 1 (A3): These photos have switched positions. Nos. 2 and 3 (A4 to A5): Not only have two more pictures swapped spots, but the mirror has drooped. No. 4 (A5): Whoever is in charge gets to keep his image on the wall. No. 5 (B1): The lampshade is expanding. No. 6 (B1 to C1): Curiosity may kill the mouse. Nos. 7 and 8 (B3): This party animal could hear a pin drop. No. 9 (C4 to D4): The quilt is turning orange. No. 10 (C5): This dog certainly likes his studs. No. 11 (E1 to E2): The cat has refolded his paws.

[MASTER]

Page 46: Staaay! No. 1 (A1 to B1): Slice that cantaloupe generously. No. 2 (A2): Make sure you grab the sugar bowl with two hands. No. 3 (A2 to B2): Check out the giant strawberry! No. 4 (B1 to B2): Just don't eat the grapes—they're going bad. No. 5 (B4 to D4): The puppy is inching closer to the food. No. 6 (C1 to C2): We've seeded this bagel with our logo. No. 7 (D2 to E2): It looks like this table could float away. No. 8 (D4 to E5): At least he has the dog bone to chew on.

Page 48: Water Sports Nos. 1 and 2 (A1): A swan has taken the place of the missing ducks. No. 3 (A5): A curious raccoon is moving in. No. 4 (A5 to B5): The fox's tail is even bushier. No. 5 (B3): And her jaw has opened in surprise. No. 6 (C1): The stick is riding high. No. 7 (C2): This guy has big feet. No. 8 (D3 to D4): The shore is getting rockier. No. 9 (E1): The fish is making a clean getaway. No. 10 (E2): The jaw's reflection *still* doesn't match topside. No. 11 (E2 to E3): And the reflection is being s-t-r-e-t-c-h-e-d.

Page 50: Food and Swine No. 1 (A3): The window's been subdivided. No. 2 (A4): Who's going to tell him he's lost his wig? No. 3 (A4 to A5): This door gets high marks. No. 4 (A5 to B5): The paper towels are solid to the core. No. 5 (A5): The rhubarb's getting a little stalky. No. 6 (C2 to C3): The railing is shrinking. No. 7 (C4): His shirttails are too long. No. 8 (C5): The door is becoming unhinged. No. 9 (D1): The new bricks are longer. No. 10 (D3): This little piggie is splotch impaired. No. 11 (E1): Someone's been tugging on the rug. No. 12 (E5): When did he find time to change his shoes?

Page 52: Just Call Him Spike The jaws in photo No. 4 will catch more dinners.

Page 53: A Mother's Work Is Never Done In photo No. 6, Mom has one more mouth to feed.

Page 54: Choose Me! No. 1 (A3): The kitty logo is taking a spin. No. 2 (B3): The net is changing colors. No. 3 (B5): She's put on her favorite fish earring. Nos. 4 and 5 (C2): There's a brand-new turtle in town and this fish is green with envy. No. 6 (D1): You've heard of "once in a blue fish," haven't you? Nos. 7 and 8 (D4): This active little goldfish really gets around, but the neon tetra looks like a fish out of water. No. 9 (D5): Her top has an extra paw print. No. 10 (E4): Turtles of a feather swim together.

Page 56: Off and Running Nos. 1 and 2 (B1 to B2): Her arm is lower, and she's lost the blue wristband. No. 3 (B3): 88 marks the spot. No. 4 (C2 to C3): Now, that's a tail! No. 5 (C3): The pole climbs higher. No. 6 (D1): The tunnel is turning blue. No. 7 (D4): His foot has cleared the hurdle. No. 8 (E5): That's a big red stripe.

Page 58: Panda-monium Nos. 1 and 2 (A4): Now that the branch is bigger, an owl has moved in. No. 3 (B1): Uh-oh, someone's cut the rope. No. 4 (B3): Somehow the pipe is just floating. No. 5 (B4): Two windows are now one. No. 6 (C3): You'll flip over the scar on the tree. No. 7 (C5): When the mask turns yellow, replace it! No. 8 (E1): This guy is nosing his way forward. No. 9 (E2): Don't sit down on the wobbly chair! No. 10 (E3 to E4): The panda has spun around. No. 11 (E5): She'd better be careful not to trip on her pants leg.

Page 60: Oops! No. 1 (A4): He's surveying all the damage he's done. Nos. 2 and 3 (A5): The cubicle panels have fused, and someone's put up quite a vacation postcard. No. 4 (A5 to B5): The screen can show bigger spreadsheets now. No. 5 (B1): The phone is sliding away. No. 6 (B3): This window won't open anymore. No. 7 (C1): Remember to lock the second drawer. No. 8 (D5): Now this chair's in wheel trouble. Nos. 9 and 10 (E1): The rubber-band ball is rolling away and the wristband is very blue.

Page 61: Finding Nemo . . . No. 1 (A2): What happened to the little blue tang? Nos. 2 and 3 (A5): The clown fish is quite the faker, and someone has a new buddy. No. 4 (B3): A blue fish just splashed in. No. 5 (B5 to C5): Watch the yellow guy skedaddle. No. 6 (C1): Is he red with white stripes or white with red stripes? No. 7 (D1 to D2): Eels are certainly slippery characters. No. 8 (D1 to E1): A clown fish dives deep. No. 9 (D2): A sea horse spins around. No. 10 (D5): This barracuda wants a free lunch. No. 11 (E3 to E4): Another fish is on the move. No. 12 (E5): That fish must have been frightened off by the barracuda.

Page 62: You From Around Here? No. 1 (A4 to B5): These pyramids have traded places. Nos. 2, 3, and 4 (B2): The little pyramid's flipped, the headdress is now blue, and the camel has lost by a nose. No. 5 (B5): A camel has wandered off. No. 6 (C3 to D4): No sitting down on the job! No. 7 (D3 to E3): Camels of the world, unite; you have nothing to lose but your chains. Nos. 8, 9, and 10 (D5): The blanket is missing a blue stripe, the tassel is hanging low, and the tail is at four o'clock.

Page 64: Clowning Around No. 1 (A4 to A5): The balloon has done an about-face. No. 2 (B2 to B3): The tent is sporting more pink fringe. No. 3 (B4): The clown needs a haircut. Nos. 4 and 5 (C1 to D1): Dog may be on the menu tonight, and the house cat has scatted. Nos. 6 and 7 (C4): The dog is trying on a new face, and his flower has a heart of red. Nos. 8 and 9 (C5): The doggie's lead has been cut, and someone is painting the wooden spool red. No. 10 (E1): This cone must be chicken. No. 11 (E2 to E3): The black-eyed Susans have started propagating. No. 12 (E5): His sock is pretty square—actually, it's lots of squares now.

Page 66: Thundering Herd No. 1 (A5): All the commotion is attracting a lioness. Nos. 2 and 3 (B2): One of these zebras is growing a Mohawk and another has quite big ears. No. 4 (B4 to C4): This one's got a swollen head. No. 5 (C2): His nose is a bit brown. No. 6 (C3): Did you spot his golden eye? No. 7 (C5): The stripes are being crosshatched. No. 8 (D3): And these stripes are merging. No. 9 (E1): The croc has vanished. No. 10 (E4 to E5): Or has he? What's that under the water?

Page 68: He's Got a Thick Hide No. 1 (A1): The post has turned around. Nos. 2 and 3 (A2): This post is still growing, and the guide is shaking his head. No. 4 (A4): It's another bad hair day. No. 5 (A5): The vulture is soaring around and around the thermal. No. 6 (B1): The board's a safety hazard. No. 7 (B2): The hook has rotated upward. No. 8 (B3): And the handle is a bit too long. No. 9 (B4): The seat has lost a strut. No. 10 (C2): This elephant has an angry glint in his eye. No. 11 (C4 to D4): The belly band must have broken. No. 12 (D1): Her pants are all purple now.

Page 70: See Spot Run, Sort Of No. 1 (A1): Danger, danger, the white tubes are multiplying. No. 2 (A5): Let's reverse the barn and tree. No. 3 (B1): The cow's lead is behind her. Nos. 4 and 5 (B2): She's got a bigger tag now, but she's lost a spot. No. 6 (B3): The boy's hair grows very fast. No. 7 (B4): Grandfather has an extra rivet on his overalls. No. 8 (C3): Half of the pail's handle has been snipped off. No. 9 (D2 to E2): The dog is wagging his tail. Nos. 10 and 11 (D3): The dog's collar needs to be trimmed, and the boy has two different size boots.

Page 72: Don't Get Crabby The crab in photo No. 2 has grown an extra leg.

Page 73: Slithering Serpents In photo No. 5, the snake is showing off his tail.

Page 74: Leader of the Pack No. 1 (A3): The family's crest has turned around. No. 2 (B2): During the night, they moved a few doors up the street. No. 3 (B4): The gardener has trimmed a little too much from this tree. Nos. 4 and 5 (C2): Her hair is longer now, and her blouse has more embroidered flowers. No. 6 (C3): His shorts have been let down. No. 7 (D2): She's going to have to

look for the shoe she lost along the way. No. 8 (D2 to D3): The bricks on the staircase have joined forces.

Page 76: These Ruins Need Fixing

3	1
6	2
4	5

Page 77: A Ruff One

3	5
6	1
2	4

Page 78: It's Lunchtime No. 1 (A1): A pelican has flown the coop. No. 2 (A3): All this attention from her chicks is giving mom quite a big head. No. 3 (A4 to A5): This bird is winging his way. No. 4 (B3): When her eyes turn orange, she's all out of fish. Nos. 5 and 6 (B5): The twig is ready to sprout now, and the little bird has swiveled around. No. 7 (D1): The yellow leaf has been inflated. No. 8 (D2): A heron is trying his luck at fishing. No. 9 (D2 to E2): She's standing on one leg. No. 10 (D4): Her meals must be nutritious—take a look at how fast this chick's wing is growing. No. 11 (E2): This ant is a leaf-crawler.

[EXPERT]

Page 82: One Horse Power No. 1 (C1): The rear window's canopy has flapped away. Nos. 2 and 3 (C2): A red stripe is now yellow, and the interior of the cabin has grown opaque. No. 4 (C3): My, what a long finger. No. 5 (C4 to C5): The horse has perked up his ear. No. 6 (D1 to D2): One of these shafts is not the same. No. 7 (D4): The traces have broken their chains. No. 8 (E1): These rocks are growing. No. 9 (E1 to E5): Either the road is falling away or everyone is floating— no, we're pretty sure it's the road. No. 10 (E2): Did anyone find a broken spoke? No. 11 (E3): That's a mega-hoof. No. 12 (E3 to E4): A back leg is starting to disappear. No. 13 (E4): He's put his right foot out in front.

Page 84: Snakes in the Grass No. 1 (A2): The butterfly is flitting away. No. 2 (A5): The diagonal stick has moved closer. No. 3 (A5 to B5): A leaf is trying to hide the snake. No. 4 (B1 to C1): Now this fruit looks ripe. No. 5 (C4): The snake is bigger than it looked. No. 6 (E1 to E2): He's just slithering along. No. 7 (E2): Keep watching the little ant that could. No. 8 (E4): This frog has one blue eye.

Page 86: Don't Feed the Bears No 1 (A2): The bus has an extra safety light—it needs a few hundred more. No. 2 (A2 to B2): Look into this mirror at your own risk. No. 3 (A4): Maybe he just wants to shake hands. No. 4 (A5): Spell-check! Anyone have a dictionary handy? No. 5 (B1): This grille can gulp a lot more air now. Nos. 6 and 7 (B2): Okay, who bit off the mirror's support *and* the red light? No. 8 (B3): He's lost his sunny smile. No. 9 (B4): This tour is all yours. No. 10 (D5): Someone's bolted more metal to the rear of the bus. No. 11 (E1 to E2): He's really quite leggy, isn't he? No. 12 (E4): One of the tire treads is missing—don't everyone look at the bear.

Page 88: Idita-ready? No. 1 (A1): Her helmet is turning blue. No. 2 (A5 to B5): All these leaves are heading for a fall. No. 3 (B1 to C1): Her sled needs a better support system. No. 4 (B2 to C2): Bigger brakes make for less road kill. No. 5 (C1): Watch out for the big wheel. No. 6 (C4 to D5): This dog may not have been born this way, but now he's running free. No. 7 (C4 to E5): Without a harness, he's also floating away. No. 8 (C5): And he's stopped wagging his tongue. No. 9 (E1): Grass grows fast around here. No. 10 (E5): He's putting his best foot forward.

Page 90: Hands Off My Food No. 1 (A1 to B1): The black rings are climbing up the tail. No. 2 (A3): With a nose like this, he must be the Pinocchio of lemurs. No. 3 (A5): Someone's dropped a carrot. Dibs! No. 4 (C3): This guy's had a trendy Hollywood nose job. No. 5 (C3 to D3): Long fingers are better for grabbing. No. 6 (C4): His eyes are green with envy. No. 7 (D1): Watch the tail wag. No. 8 (D4): The worm is inching along. No. 9 (D4 to D5): The cucumber is still growing. No. 10 (E1): He's checking you out—and he's none too happy with what he sees. No. 11 (E2 to E3): The logo is now blue. No. 12 (E2 to E4): The base of the bowl has lost some notches. No. 13 (E5): This curious chap is popping his head up.

Page 92: Swimming Lessons No. 1 (A3 to B4): Momma's head is swelling with pride. No. 2 (A5): The red leaf is drifting into view. No. 3 (B5): The frog has turned his back on the world. No. 4 (C1): The duckling's head has lost its stripe. No. 5 (C2): He's wide-eyed about how new everything is. No. 6 (C3): The beak is blushing pink. No. 7 (C4): He's going through a growth spurt. No. 8 (D5): The leaf is twirling in the water. No. 9 (E5): This duckling paddles to a different drummer.

Page 93: Shell Game No. 1 (A3): The shirt hangs low. No. 2 (A4): The satchel's tag is seeing red. No. 3 (A4 to B4): This microphone can pick up the slightest whisper. No. 4 (A5 to B5): It must be spring; the twig is all leafed out. No. 5 (C1 to D2): This tortoise is not camera shy. No. 6 (C3): Now the photographer can't count past nine. No. 7 (C5 to D5): His shorts aren't so short. No. 8 (D5): Did his strap break—or did something eat it? No. 9 (E2): This hardback looks very pretty in pink. No. 10 (E5): Some of the rock has suddenly broken away.

Page 94: Farm Fresh No. 1 (A3 to A4): The ivy has been trimmed. No. 2 (B3): There seem to be some doubts about this sale. No. 3 (C3): Are they selling plants or planners? No. 4 (C5): This dog has a great nose. No. 5 (D1): The front pot has enlarged just a bit. No. 6 (D5): The trunk of this birch sapling is growing back. No. 7 (E2): The hat has a longer ribbon now. Nos. 8 and 9 (E4): Both the skirt and sock have gotten longer.

Page 96: You Looking at Me? In photo No. 6, the gecko has made a four-point landing.

Page 97: And Baby Makes Three The baby's horns haven't grown yet in photo No. 1.

Page 98: Walk This Way Nos. 1 and 2 (A2): He's changed his turban, and the window is now sealed off. No. 3 (A4): The view through this window has turned over. No. 4 (A4 to A5): This little window has gotten bigger. No. 5 (B2): The elephant has changed his license plate. Nos. 6 and 7 (B4): The mahout uses his big finger to point the way, while a macaque has popped up in back. No. 8 (C4 to D5): Somebody's really pulling his leg. No. 9 (C5): Another macaque has joined the troop. No. 10 (D3): The trunk is now a lefty. No. 11 (D4 to E4): The tail has swished. No. 12 (E2): The tail's shadow is also on the move.

Page 100: Last One In Is Whale Food No. 1 (A5): The homeward-bound petrel is flapping his wings. No. 2 (B1): Like a movie star from a bygone era, this penguin "vants to be alone." No. 3 (B2 to B3): A mamma and baby orca are swimming for snacks. No. 4 (B4): Part of this iceberg now sleeps with the fishes. No. 5 (C1): A seal has slipped into the sea. No. 6 (C3 to D3): This boy's still growing. Nos. 7, 8, and 9 (C5): Papa orca is catching up with his family, this penguin feels like dancing, but his friend can't bear to watch. No. 10 (D2): A dapper bird has donned formal attire. No. 11 (D3): He's gone for a swim.

Page 101: Little Nipper Napping No. 1 (A1): A curious fawn sidles up to the boy. No. 2 (B5 to C5): When he wakes up, he should put on matching shoes. No. 3 (C2): The towel has blanched. No. 4 (C3 to C4): One brave rabbit hopes for table scraps. No. 5 (C4 to C5): This picnic table needs a good carpenter. No. 6 (C5): The planks on the bench had an urge to merge. No. 7 (D1): Don't sit down at this end! No. 8 (E1): A cat is on the prowl. Nos. 9 and 10 (E3): The bird has turned but keeps a wary eye on the cat, while the strap has lost its adjuster. Nos. 11 and 12 (E4): As the bench loses its bolt, the squirrel munches nuts.

Page 102: Summertime . . . No. 1 (A1): This gull is the winner. No. 2 (A2): Someone is walking on the pier. No. 3 (A3): The boat has turned around. Nos. 4 and 5 (A4): While the speedboat races away, the red float keeps multiplying. Nos. 6 and 7 (B2): A new gull has found a perch, and a pile has lost some height. Nos. 8 and 9 (B3): While the pile rises up, a duck settles in for a nap. No. 10 (B5 to C5): The gull is restless. No. 11 (C5): You can really lean back in the deck chair now. Nos. 12 and 13 (D1 to E1): These gulls are fleeing for their lives. No. 14 (D2): Who will save the birds by belling the cat? No. 15 (E1): The deck needs some minor repair.

[GENIUS]

Page 106: Mr. Zippy No. 1 (A1 to B1): A deer lurks in the woods. Nos. 2 and 3 (A2): One tree has flipped, while another has magically appeared. No. 4 (A5): Who chopped down the not-cherry tree? Nos. 5 and 6 (B4): As he cranes his neck, his eye changes color. No. 7 (C1): Leaf litter has covered up the log. No. 8 (C2): The shell is being retouched. No. 9 (C4): The stick is now behind the log. No. 10 (D3): The leg has an extra scale. No. 11 (D5): This leaf has LIFE in its veins. Nos. 12 and 13 (E1): While the top leaf curls, a mouse hides underneath. No. 14 (E3): The moss has thinned in front of his leg. No. 15 (E4 to E5): A twig is poking up.

Page 108: Wool Gathering No. 1 (A2): This is the post with the most. No. 2 (A3 to A4): Now his cap matches his scarf. No. 3 (A4): His shirt has been redesigned. Nos. 4 and 5 (A4 to A5): A boy is sneaking a peek at the fair, and this gent has traded up in hats. No. 6 (B1 to B2): They're stringing more barbed wire. No. 7 (B3): Her skirt is fancier. No. 8 (B4): What's he looking at now? No. 9 (B4 to B5): His braid is floating. No. 10 (B5 to E5): She's stepped forward. No. 11 (C1): Don't tug on her ear and it won't get any bigger. No. 12 (C3): A poncho flaps in front of the wire. No. 13 (D1): She's lifting her foot. No. 14 (D2): The pole floats in the air. No. 15 (E4 to E5): The poncho hangs low. No. 16 (E5): This lamb follows the flock.

Page 110: Run Away! No. 1 (A2): The spear's binding is new. No. 2 (A3): His hat's top flap has fluttered behind the red one. No. 3 (A4 to A5): The flag blows in the breeze. No. 4 (B1): The cuff is longer. No. 5 (B4 to B5): The parapet needs repair. Nos. 6 and 7 (C3): His sleeve is in front of the axe shaft, while his shirt has dropped a star. No. 8 (D2): The black horse is lifting his head. No. 9 (D3): The starry patch has spun around. No. 10 (D4): The blade is missing. No. 11 (D5): Who cut the straps short? No. 12 (E3): A stirrup has fallen by the wayside. No. 13 (E4): His boot size keeps going up. No. 14 (E5): When he flares his nostrils, his mouth closes.

Page 111: Practical Yoke No. 1 (A5): This horn looks dangerous. Nos. 2 and 3 (B1): Part of another horn has vanished and the yoke has been extended. Nos. 4 and 5 (B2): One pole is growing and the horn slipped behind the yoke.

No. 6 (B5): His ear is just a little short. No. 7 (C2): A distant tree is missing. No. 8 (C4): This beast of burden is getting a little nosy. No. 9 (C5 to D5): Now his clothes match. No. 10 (D1): This tree just sprouted right up. No. 11 (D3): The plow's handle has broken. Nos. 12, 13, and 14 (D4): The diagonal crossbeam has slipped behind, the hut has been downsized, and the water buffalo has taken a step backward. No. 15 (D5): He's lost his reflection. No. 16 (E1): The frog has swum away.

Page 112: Monkey on His Back No. 1 (A1): The *T* in PICTURE has blown its top. No. 2 (A2 to C2): The panels have fused. No. 3 (A2): Two binders have joined forces. Nos. 4 and 5 (A3): The file folder is a little blue, and the red binder is has started to grow. No. 6 (A4 to B4): The magnet is now purple. Nos. 7 and 8 (A4 to A5): This wall has been jacked up and the calendar's turning green. Nos. 9, 10, and 11 (B3 to B4): He's swapped out two family photos and changed a sticky note. No. 12 (B3 to C3): The pages on this screen look strangely familiar. No. 13 (B4): He needs a trim in the back. No. 14 (C1): The file folder has an extra stripe. No. 15 (C5): The mouse is on the move. No. 16 (D1): His pen has had a dye job. No. 17 (D2): This envelope is for oversize memos. No. 18 (D4): The baboon has restless leg syndrome. No. 19 (D5 to E5): He's got a yo-yo of a tail. No. 20 (E4): The chair is about to tumble down.

Page 114: Launching No. 1 (A2 to A4): One of these cables has snapped. No. 2 (A4): She's changed her top. No. 3 (A5): The safety chain is gone. No. 4 (B2): That's one big ball. No. 5 (B4 to B5): His flipper is flapping. Nos. 6 and 7 (B5): She's got great gams, and the concrete slab has slid forward. No. 8 (C1): Now they can shine more light on the subject. No. 9 (C2): The red pole has lost its way. Nos. 10 and 11 (C3): He's copied his friend's face, and a twin has grabbed a seat. No. 12 (C5): A pole is missing. No. 13 (D2): The staircase has been extended. No. 14 (E1): So that's where his ducky ended up. No. 15 (E1 to E5): The pool appears to be tilting.

Page 116: Crowded House No. 1 (A1): Momma's got a brand-new basket. No. 2 (A2): The handles are slipping down. Nos. 3 and 4 (A4): The light panel is migrating upward and one switch has disappeared. No. 5 (A5): We wonder what the dogs think of this photo. Nos. 6 and 7 (B2): Her hair band is now blue and the bottle holds more water. No. 8 (B3): The mug is a mirror image of its former self. No. 9 (B4): Her watch band needs a little tightening. No. 10 (B4 to B5): The ponytail is now shorter. Nos. 11 and 12 (B5): Her seat back is taller and a drawer has lost a knob. No. 13 (C2): The dog's head has lost its stripe. No. 14 (C3 to C4): So have her pants. No. 15 (C4): This dog has donned blue contacts. No. 16 (C4 to D5): The other has mutant ears. No. 17 (E5): The bed has lost a cross.

Page 118: Knock, Knock—Anyone Home? No. 1 (A1 to B1): The tree has grown an extra limb. No. 2 (A3): Fess up. Who cut this tree down? Nos. 3 and 4 (B3): On the cabin's roof the big spikes are winning out over the little ones, and the post's roof is mossy green. No. 5 (B3 to C4): The window has fewer panes. Nos. 6 and 7 (C1): The bird house has a new opening, and

they're growing the rare blue tulip. Nos. 8 and 9 (C2): The latch has been lowered and this bird house has no exit. Nos. 10 and 11 (C3): The bell now hangs from a longer cord and the shutter is drooping. Nos. 12, 13, and 14 (C4): The birds have enlarged their own window, the trellis has two longer stakes, and the checkerboard is being flooded with maroon. No. 15 (D1 to D2): The frog tile is expanding. No. 16 (D2 to E2): You've heard of blowfish? This is a blow-cat. He puffs up when he's hunting. No. 17 (D3): There's an extra tulip hiding here. No. 18 (D4 to E4): The cat's younger brother is on a snipe hunt too. No. 19 (D5): The rustic bird house is being expanded into a barn.

[LIFE CLASSICS]

Page 122: Tweetie Birds No. 1 (A1): A parakeet's coming in for a landing. No. 2 (A5): This bird is approaching from the right. No. 3 (B2): He's sliding along his perch. No. 4 (B4): Don't let the birds play on the swing until it's been repaired. No. 5 (D1 to E1): The toy mouse has shuffled to the right. No. 6 (D3): A rung has broken off the ladder. No. 7 (D4): The barbell is an itsy-bitsy bit longer. Nos. 8 and 9 (E3): The toy bird has reversed itself and two real birds are getting cozy.

Page 124: Who Needs a Spoon? No. 1 (B1): The back of this chair is extendable. No. 2 (B5): A rooster struts across the backyard shadows. No. 3 (C2 to C3): Now the bowl can hold more scoops of ice cream. No. 4 (C3): There's an extra bowl for anyone who wants seconds. No. 5 (D2): Our name has magically appeared on her dress. No. 6 (D2 to E2): She's pulled her sock up. No. 7 (D3 to D4): Just in case, the table now has extra bracing. No. 8 (E5): The raccoon is about to get a big surprise.

Page 125: Don't Spook the Ponies No. 1 (A4): The electricians have installed a new lamp. No. 2 (A5 to C5): Now the studio has a Dutch door. No. 3 (B2 to B3): This lamp hangs lower. No. 4 (B3 to C3): The horse's face has grown. No. 5 (B5 to C5): They're working on a new horse over here. No. 6 (C4): The board has been lengthened. No. 7 (D2): So has this pole. No. 8 (D4): The table legs have lost a brace. No. 9 (D5): The cat seems a little shorter. No. 10 (E3): Someone left an extra can on the floor.

Page 126: Making a Splash No. 1 (B2): The audience is filling up with clones. No. 2 (B2 to B3): As he burst through the hoop, an unexplained release of delta radiation caused the dolphin to experience an unusual growth spurt. No. 3 (B3): This woman has returned to her seat just in time. No. 4 (B3 to B4): Apparently, they've sold off all but one of the studios. No. 5 (B5): The flagpole has skittered to the side. No. 6 (C1): This couple looks kind of familiar . . . but smaller. Hmm. No. 7 (C2): She's recrossed her legs. No. 8 (C4 to C5): He's making quite a splash with his tail. No. 9 (D1 to E1): They're setting up an extra bracket just in time for the next show.

Page 128: A Maxi Lube Job No. 1 (A3): The sign has been revised. No. 2 (A4): Who closed the window? No. 3 (A5): They tiled over a small opening. No. 4 (B1): The auto shop will only do one repair per car. No. 5 (B3): Bored with changing signs, now they just steal them. No. 6 (C1 to D2): This nice old lady wants to know what's going on. No. 7 (C5): These two have taken a careful step back. No. 8 (D1): The truck has a new number. No. 9 (D5): The manhole was moved to protect delicate elephant feet. Nos. 10 and 11 (E5): The elephant is lifting her trunk, which makes this man a little nervous.

Page 130: Weighty Matters No. 1 (A1 to D1): The chair has been stretched sideways, along with its reflection. No. 2 (A2): It has also lost its back. No. 3 (B2 to B4): The pan is just a bit shallower. No. 4 (C1 to E1): This is quite a tail. Nos. 5 and 6 (C3): The pole is now behind the towel and the dial begins at 24. No. 7 (C4 to C5): The table leg is a little longer. No. 8 (D2): His restless foot is in front of the scale. No. 9 (E3): It's legal to use this scale in stores now. No. 10 (E5): That's one big tile.

Page 132: Howdy, Pardners No. 1 (A2 to A3): The store is under new management but it's still in the family. No. 2 (B1 to C4): Honey, they shrunk the sign. No. 3 (C1 to C2): The gas pump has more nozzle. Nos. 4 and 5 (C2): Someone's screwed in an extra lightbulb, and the boy has replaced his hat. No. 6 (C4): The sign has dropped a period. No. 7 (C5 to D5): The rider's arm has swung backward. Nos. 8 and 9 (C5): LIFE now sells gasoline *and* books, while, brick by brick, the chimney reaches skyward. No. 10 (D1): The cases of bottles are stacking up. No. 11 (D2): He's lost his stirrup. Nos. 12 and 13 (D3): A man has appeared out of the shadows, and the waiter is standing tall. No. 14 (E3 to E4): This horse casts no shadow. No. 15 (E5): And his back legs are just ridiculous.

Page 134: Herd Instinct No. 1 (A1): One of these flags flaps against the wind. No. 2 (A2): Two windows have swapped places. No. 3 (A3): This flag is shy a star. No. 4 (B1): These two guys look alike. No. 5 (B3): Please don't get stung by the BEE. No. 6 (B4): Somebody get this statue a barber. No. 7 (B5): His index finger is a little too long. No. 8 (C1): The wall has two new slots. No. 9 (C2 to D2): The planter and shrub have come up a little short. No. 10 (C3): Tourists must be tugging on his leg—it's really been stretched out. No. 11 (D2): This sheep is sporting a new ear. No. 12 (E4): The sheep dog is nipping on a new flank.

Coming Attractions

Here's a small sneak preview of our next puzzle book, *Holidays!*
It's coming soon to a bookstore near you.

8
changes

KEEP
SCORE

☐
☐
☐
☐
☐
☐
☐
☐

⧗
4min 30sec

A — B — C — D — E

1   2   3   4   5